ONE-BLOCK
WONDERS

ONE FABRIC, ONE SHAPE, ONE-OF-A-KIND QUILTS

MAXINE ROSENTHAL

C&T PUBLISHING

C&T Publishing, Inc.

Text © 2005 Maxine Rosenthal

Artwork © 2005 C&T Publishing, Inc.

Publisher: Amy Marson

Editorial Director: Gailen Runge

Acquisitions Editor: Jan Grigsby

Editor: Cyndy Lyle Rymer

Technical Editors: Helen Young Frost, Susan Nelson

Copyeditor/Proofreader: Wordfirm, Inc.

Design Director/Cover & Book Designer: Christina D. Jarumay

Illustrator: Kiera Lofgreen

Production Assistant: Kiera Lofgreen

Photography: Diane Pedersen and Luke Mulks unless otherwise noted

Published by C&T Publishing, Inc., P.O. Box 1456, Lafayette, CA 94549

Library of Congress Cataloging-in-Publication Data

Rosenthal, Maxine

One-block wonders : one fabric, one shape, one-of-a-kind quilts / Maxine Rosenthal.

   p. cm.

Includes index.

ISBN-13: 978-1-57120-322-9 (paper trade)

ISBN-10: 1-57120-322-2 (paper trade)

1. Patchwork–Patterns. 2. Quilting. 3. Kaleidoscope quilts. I. Title.

TT835.R674 2006

746.46'041–dc22

2005018623

Printed in China

10 9 8 7 6 5 4 3 2 1

Purple and Green Cubes, 55˝ × 69˝, machine pieced and quilted by the author. This early quilt features cubes: some are hollow, and some are solid but open on one side. It is interesting to come up with different ways to show dimension on a flat surface.

ACKNOWLEDGMENTS

I would like to thank many people who have helped me along the way.

Penny Simison, who never lost faith in me and who kept me writing and rewriting and rewriting.

My good friends Meg Devine and Joy Pelzmann, who have used my ideas, often showing me what else could be done, and who have enjoyed looking at new fabric with the notion of possibilities.

My daughter, Petra, who has accepted so many quilts even though she lives in Southern California and has probably never needed any blankets on her bed.

DEDICATION

To Stan

Petra's Chickens, 65″ × 64″, machine pieced and quilted by the author. This quilt was made for my daughter, Petra, and features another favorite chicken fabric.

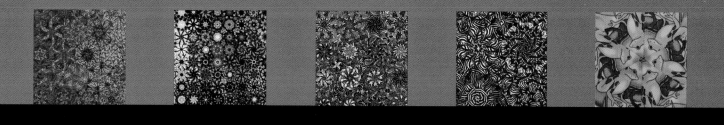

CONTENTS

CHAPTER **1** Introduction ...**6**

    Supplies You Will Need ...**8**

CHAPTER **2** The Star Player: Fabric ...**10**

    What's in the Background? ...**11**

    Stripes Versus Swirls ...**12**

    Large Is Good ...**13**

    Yardage Amounts ...**17**

CHAPTER **3** Prepare the Fabric ...**18**

    Cutting Repeats ...**19**

CHAPTER **4** Hexagon Blocks ...**26**

    Cutting Process ...**27**

    Sewing the Hexagons ...**29**

    Designing With Hexagons ...**32**

    Shape and Size of the Final Quilt ...**40**

    Sewing the Quilt Top Together ...**40**

    One-of-a-Kind Quilt With Hexagons ...**44**

CHAPTER **5** Octagon Blocks ...**46**

    Cutting Process ...**47**

    Sewing the Octagons ...**49**

    Designing With Octagons ...**53**

    Shape and Size of the Final Quilt ...**56**

    Sensational Squares ...**56**

    Sewing the Quilt Top Together ...**58**

    One-of-a-Kind Quilt With Octagons ...**60**

CHAPTER **6** Borders ...**62**

    Border Variations ...**63**

    Measure the Quilt Top ...**63**

    Narrow Accent Borders ...**64**

CHAPTER **7** What to Do With Extra Kaleidoscopes ...**66**

    Table Runner With Octagon Kaleidoscopes ...**67**

    Pot Holders ...**68**

About the Author ...**71**

Index ...**72**

1

Introduction

Zebras, 64″ × 71″, machine pieced and quilted by the author.

Fabric for *Zebras*

Fabric for hexagonal blocks

You will love this unusual method of designing and creating quilts. Instead of starting with a particular pattern or design and then trying to find fabric that will fit that pattern, this approach begins with the fabric: the fabric is the key element. Kaleidoscope blocks—each one unique—are produced by aligning the printed design on several layers of fabric and then cutting and sewing triangles together. Just as the mirrors in a kaleidoscope reflect and repeat an image, each triangle repeats color and pattern to create a new design for each block. Once all the blocks are made, you begin to design your quilt.

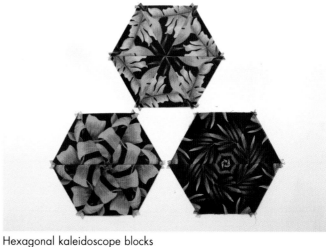

Hexagonal kaleidoscope blocks

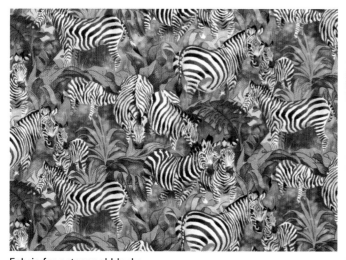

Fabric for octagonal blocks

Octagonal kaleidoscope blocks

This is a serendipitous and adventurous approach to design. One piece of fabric does all the work, because the fabric contains all the colors and all the design elements. You cut and sew one shape—with triangles forming hexagons or octagons—and then design with these kaleidoscopic blocks. Because the quilts feature one repeated block, design merely involves playing with colors and shapes within the kaleidoscopes. The quilt you produce has more energy and movement than the original fabric.

This is a very forgiving process—there is so much motion and pattern in the quilt that mistakes are rarely seen. The idea is to relax and enjoy each kaleidoscope block as it comes to life and the quilt design unfolds.

The following chapters help you find suitable fabric, layer it, and create your unique quilt top using hexagons or octagons. Purchasing and layering the fabric—steps that are common to both hexagon and octagon blocks—are presented first. The elements of design for hexagons and octagons are similar, but because the shapes are so different, the sewing process for each is covered in separate chapters.

There are not very many rules. It is hard to say exactly what size the quilt will turn out to be. The size depends on the size of the borders; the number of hexagons or octagons in the quilt; and whether the quilt is long and thin, almost square, or divided into two or more panels with borders around each.

I have made many baby quilts using this process. In my imagination, I can see a child recovering from the flu, sitting in bed, bored and weary. The quilt captures her attention. She searches for the exact place in the fabric that produced each kaleidoscope. Boredom has been changed to a game that whiles away the afternoon.

Supplies You Will Need

As a quilter, you probably already own all or most of the tools required to make a one-block wonder.

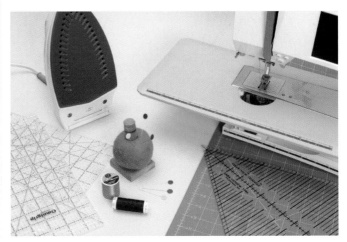
Tools

- Rotary cutting equipment: You will need a self-healing mat, long and short rulers, a square ruler for squaring the blocks, and a 45mm- or 60mm-blade rotary cutter. It is a good idea to insert a new blade into the rotary cutter to ease the work of cutting six or eight layers at one time.

- A 60° ruler (optional): Though this ruler is helpful when cutting hexagons, it is not necessary. Most rulers have a 60° line on them that you can use instead.

- Flower pins: These pins lie flat and do not shift when you are cutting.

- Sewing machine in good working order with a ¼″ foot

- Thread

- Iron

- Design wall: This wall is indispensable for looking at a design from a distance. When you design on a floor, some things are closer to your eye than others; on a wall, everything is nearly equidistant. You can actually step back to view your quilt, making it easy to see what is right and wrong about your design as you progress.

I improvised a wonderful design wall with batting and insulation. I used fanfold insulation because it folded into a size that fit into my car so I could get it home from the home improvement store.

I screwed the insulation to the wall, covering an entire wall with this lovely pink stuff. Then I opened a queen-size cotton batting, put it in the dryer for 10 minutes to get out the creases, and nailed the batting to the insulation. I now have a very large wall on which to design my kaleidoscope wonders.

My friend used two sheets of insulation. (She has a larger car than I do and could get them home!) She taped the two sheets together, side by side, and then attached the batting. However, she did not attach the insulation to the wall. Instead, she propped the sheets against it. Because the design wall leans against the wall, the blocks never fall off. She keeps this design wall in her living room and considers it revolving art. People love to visit and see what she is working on.

Detail of *Zebras*

2

The Star Player:
Fabric

African Veldt, 70″ × 76″, machine pieced and quilted by the author. So many animals, and all from one fabric. I tried to arrange them in color order, not the way they are in real life.

There are so many wonderful fabrics in quilt and fabric stores. Because only one fabric is used to create the kaleidoscope blocks, there are a few considerations to help make this process successful.

Choose a fabric that features your favorite colors. If you like the colors of the fabric, you will enjoy making the quilt. My favorite color is red. I almost never need to walk down the brown aisle in any store.

What's in the Background?

Select a fabric with a minimal amount of background. Too much background produces blocks with little design and mostly background. A fabric with several smaller animals or design elements spaced apart from each other is not a good choice either.

It is easiest to work with a background that is not a solid color. For example, fish in a raging sea work better than flowers on a black background. The background in the fish fabric adds movement and interest.

Background with movement

Fabric with small design elements

Plain background

Detail of *African Veldt*

Stripes Versus Swirls

Avoid fabric with stripes or straight lines that run parallel or perpendicular to the selvage; this includes boxes with edges that are parallel to the selvage. Stripes may be lovely, but when you cut the fabric and sew it back together, you will have to match those stripes, which requires precision and care. Instead, choose a fabric with a swirling form, because the swirls will never be expected to meet at the seam.

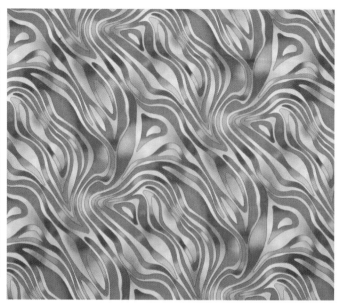

Fabric with swirling design

Fabric with straight lines

Blocks from fabric with swirling design

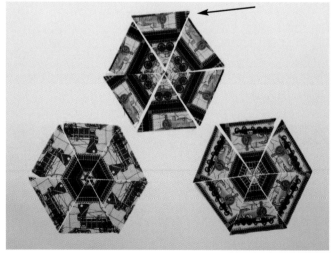

Blocks from fabric with straight lines

Some fabric designs that give the illusion of movement work very well for these one-block wonders. For example, leaves printed with straight veins and smooth sides can look stiff; leaves with scalloped edges and curling tips seem to move. Fabric that features this movement or feeling of flow is more interesting than fabric with plain lines.

Straight leaves versus leaves with movement

Kaleidoscope blocks from large print

Although any leaf can be beautiful, one that is larger and that has more curls is more interesting.

Large Is Good

The larger the print, the less the finished blocks will look like the original fabric. This is the result you want! When you cut up these large prints and put them back together, the kaleidoscopes they form lose the original motif to create their own new motif. You can then design with the lines and colors of the original fabric.

Notice that fabric is printed with the designs repeating both horizontally and vertically. If the fabric repeat is very frequent or every few inches, it will produce the same kaleidoscopes over and over again. Look for a fabric with as much variety as possible—this variety will help when you are ready to design your quilt. (By "more variety" I mean a fabric with a large repeat.)

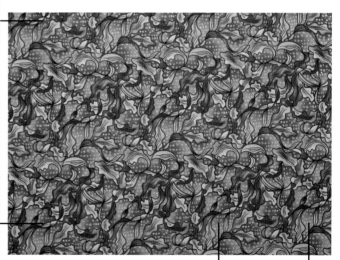

Horizontal and vertical repeat

Original fabric with large print

Fabric with large animals or floral prints, or even people, makes an interesting kaleidoscope because there is something recognizable within the kaleidoscope, such as fish tails, lions' noses, car tires, or a cowboy's hand waving as he rides a bucking bronco.

Mirrors on fabric

Limit the number of colors in the fabric. It is much easier to design with two or three colors than with eight or nine.

Fabric with too many colors

The *Persian Carpet* quilt includes variations of one color, but overall, it is only one color. It is amazing how much variety you can produce from a single color in the original fabric.

Fabric for *Persian Carpet*

Detail of *Persian Carpet*

Persian Carpet, 70″ × 74″, machine pieced and quilted by the author. This was another attempt at subtlety, but it was also a challenge to create something out of a fabric that did not look like it would be appropriate for kaleidoscopes.

Starry Night, 55″ × 66″, machine
pieced and quilted by Joy Pelzmann.
A fabric with blue water and orange
fish was transformed into an image of
a night sky with sparkling stars.

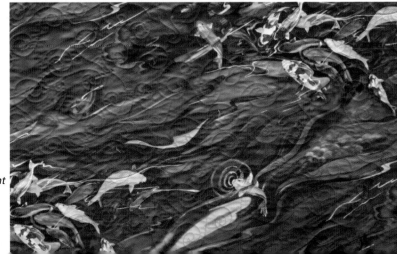

Fabric for *Starry Night*

Yardage Amounts

How much fabric should you buy? There are very few rules, but there are some guidelines. The size of the quilt depends not only on how much fabric you buy, but also on how many hexagon blocks or octagon blocks you eventually use in the quilt. There always seem to be some leftovers, which are addressed in Chapter 7, What to Do With Extra Kaleidoscopes (page 66). The amount of fabric also depends on how you arrange the hexagons and on the shape of the finished quilt. It may be your intention to make several table runners rather than one quilt—it is all up to you!

■ How Much Fabric to Buy

To make a good lap-size, twin, or full-size quilt, 4½ yards for hexagon blocks or 5¾ yards for octagon blocks is enough. For a queen size or larger quilt, double those amounts to 9 yards for hexagon blocks or 11½ yards for octagon blocks.

MEASURE THE REPEAT

Measure along the selvage from the start of a design element to the point where the design appears again—this is the size of the repeat. If the distance between the repeats is 6″ to 8″, which is a short repeat, the fabric will produce a very small project. For short repeats, you can opt to buy twelve repeats instead of six if you are making hexagons, or sixteen repeats instead of eight if you are making octagons. Buying twice as many repeats as necessary means that two or more kaleidoscope designs may be identical. There are ways to avoid this (see page 29).

Larger prints usually feature a repeat about every 24″. This is the type of fabric I typically choose. Four to five yards makes a very comfortable lap quilt, and depending on the borders used, it can grow to almost any size.

Comparing the kaleidoscopes with the original fabric is fun. It is nothing short of magical to see the transformation that the original fabric has gone through. So, buy a little extra to use as a border or backing.

FOR HEXAGONS: 6 repeats at 24″ each is exactly 4 yards (24 x 6 = 144; 144/36 = 4).
Add an extra half yard or yard (4½ or 5 yards) to have a piece of the original fabric as a reference.

FOR OCTAGONS: 8 repeats at 24″ is 5⅓ yards (24 x 8 = 192; 192/36 = 5.333).
Again, add extra—5¾ or 6 yards is a good amount to buy.

OTHER GUIDELINES FOR FABRIC

The wonderful thing about making these quilts is the lack of fabric preparation. *There is no need to pre-wash the fabric.* This removes the sizing and can distort the fabric. You can begin cutting into your fabric as soon as you get it home!

Do not buy fabric from more than one bolt. Sometimes you find the perfect fabric, but there is only a yard or two on the bolt, so you go to the Internet or to another store to buy more of the same fabric. This will not work. There is no guarantee that the colors or print of the pattern are exactly the same from bolt to bolt.

Prepare the Fabric

Hot Chilies, 77˝ × 80˝, machine pieced by the author and quilted by
Runs With Scissors. This was the first quilt I did using this method. I
was astounded at what it produced and how easily it came together.

For both octagons and hexagons, take the time to prepare the fabric for ease in cutting. Leave the fabric folded as it came off the bolt—both selvages are on one side and the fold is on the other. This helps the fabric fit comfortably on the cutting board.

Cutting Repeats

The first cuts are made to separate the yardage into six or eight elements that are the same in terms of design placement. This first rough cut will be refined after all six or eight repeats are cut (six repeats for hexagons or eight repeats for octagons).

The size of the cut depends on the length of the repeat. The width is always approximately 42″, which is the width of the fabric, but the length depends on the size of the repeat. A 24″ repeat means that each cut will be made every 24″; an 8″ repeat means that each cut will be 8″ or, if you bought twice as many repeats as needed, 16″.

First cut the fabric based on the design repeats. To cut your first repeat, look along the cut edge of the fabric. Identify a design element close to the cut edge that will be easy to recognize when it next appears. Move along either the fold line or the selvages of the fabric and look for that design element again.

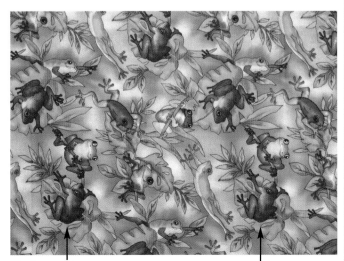

Single repeat

If your repeat is so frequent that you have doubled its number, move along to the next time you see this design element.

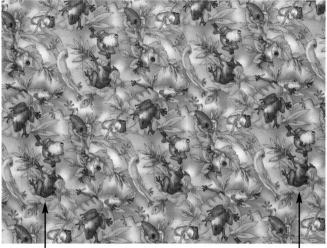

Double repeat

Steps for Cutting Repeats

1. The initial design element is at the beginning of the fabric. Cut through all layers of fabric, from selvage to selvage, just before this design element appears again. Put this piece aside. Note: This is a rough initial cut. You are not trying for perfection yet.

2. Cut the next repeat the same way so the next cut ends at the same place in the design as the first one ended. Pile this second cut on the first cut. Continue cutting until you have either 6 or 8 repeats—6 repeats for hexagons and 8 repeats for octagons.

Same design element

Cutting the next repeat

3. You now have 6 or 8 layers of fabric that are about the same. Unfold each piece and iron it to remove the center fold. Place one repeat over the next, making sure that the pattern is facing in the same direction. Do not worry if they are not exactly the same or if one is a little longer than the other.

4. You will insert 6 flower pins into the fabric, as described in the following steps:

- 2 along one selvage
- 2 on either side at about the center fold
- 2 along the other selvage

5. Starting at the corner of a selvage, look for a place where 2 design elements intersect. This intersection point should be about 1″ from the cut edge of the fabric and about 1″ from the selvage. Do not use the end of a design element as your point. As fabric is printed, the end of an element may not always be printed, but where design elements cross, they will always cross. Put a flower pin straight into the point where the elements meet.

Intersection of design elements

6. Lift the top piece of fabric, with the pin sticking into it, to reveal the next layer of fabric. Push the pin into the spot where the same 2 lines intersect on this next piece of fabric. Repeat for the remaining layers. *Count* as you go along. It is very easy not to pick up enough layers because one was folded in or did not reach the edge.

7. Leave the pin sticking straight into the fabric. Repeat Steps 5 and 6 on the other cut edge along the same selvage edge.

Insert 2 pins along the selvage.

8. There are now 2 pins sticking straight into the fabric, one at either edge of one selvage. Hold the shaft of each pin between your index finger and middle finger—holding a pin in each hand. Press the edge of each flower-pin head with your thumb. It looks awkward. It is awkward. But you really have a grip on it.

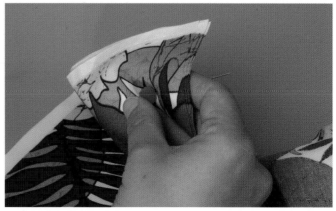

How to hold a pin

Holding 2 pins

9. Be sure to hold just the pins and let the fabric hang loose. Give a little shake with your hands to straighten the fabric.

Note: If you prewashed this fabric, it will stick together and not shake out freely.

While holding the pins, give the fabric a gentle tug away from the center. This process of aligning the fabric is the hardest task. Once you align the fabric you can relax and enjoy the rest.

10. Lay the fabric down. Check along the selvage edge and along the sides to ensure that the pattern showing in the layers is aligned. Spread apart the layers of fabric to see if the print matches.

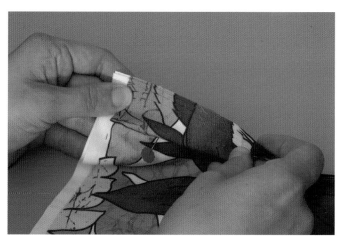

Fabric aligned

11. With the fabric resting on the table, hold the shaft of the pin in the fabric so the index and middle fingers of one hand are behind the fabric and your thumb is leaning on the front of the fabric. Do not turn this pin to secure the fabric—that would change the alignment you just worked so hard to get perfect. With your other hand, insert another flower pin into the fabric so that it slides in almost parallel to the fabric's edge. When inserting this pin, make sure it is at such a slanted angle that the pattern on each layer remains aligned. When you let go of the original pin, it should still stand straight.

Pin standing straight

If the first pin does not stand straight, pull out the second flower pin and reinsert it, trying not to shift any of the layers as you do so. On the front side of the fabric, there should be a long space of fabric between the points where the pin entered and exited; on the back side, there should be very little pin showing. This indicates that the pin is at an angle slanted enough so as not to alter the alignment of the layers of fabric.

12. Remove the pin that is sticking straight up beside the new pin.

13. Repeat Steps 11 and 12 with the other side of the selvage. You now have 2 pins securing the fabric.

14. Move down the fabric to the fold line. Put a flower pin straight in on either side along the cut edges, in the same way as in Steps 5 and 6. Again find an easily recognizable place where 2 lines of a pattern element intersect. These 2 pins will stick straight up. Hold on to them as in Step 9 and give the fabric a little shake and then tug outward to align all the layers.

Hold 2 pins at the center along the fold line.

15. Replace each pin with another flower pin as in Steps 11 and 12.

16. Repeat this entire process at the other selvage. For this step, it is easiest to turn the fabric around so the bottom selvage is at the top.

The fabric is now perfectly aligned and you have 6 pins holding the fabric in place. You can confirm this by looking at the print of the fabric along the cut edges to see that it lines up.

17. Use a rotary cutter and ruler to cut a straight edge along one side, from selvage to selvage. Only one edge needs to be cut straight. If the edge is not perfectly straight, that's OK—you will be cutting small triangles, so you don't need an edge perfectly perpendicular to the selvage.

Cutting a straight edge

Detail of *Are Those Shamrocks?*

Are Those Shamrocks? 70″ × 59″,
machine pieced by Meg Devine,
quilted by the author.

Fabric for *Are Those Shamrocks?*

Chard, 56″ × 46″, machine pieced and quilted by the author. I love the fact that the colors are not realistic. Most chard is green, but I love the blood red in the leaves. I would have loved to have used only that, but who wastes fabric?

Fabric for *Chard*

Koi Polloi, 44″ × 53″, machine pieced and quilted by Joy Pelzmann.

Fabric for *Koi Polloi*

Hexagon Blocks

Out of the Box: Hexagons and Cubes, 85″ × 72″,
machine pieced and quilted by the author.
This quilt stretched my imagination. I loved
making hollow cubes, but what if they were
to fill in and become solid? And what if they
were falling out of the quilt?

Hexagon blocks are made from triangles cut from strips. Hexagons can be any size. The aim is to use all of your purchased fabric. A 4″ strip from fabric with a 24″ repeat will divide exactly, with no fabric left over, but this assumes that every strip cut, and its alignment, will be exact. Because we are not perfect, however, it is better to have a "fudge factor" just in case. Therefore, the strips are cut 3¾″, which leaves a 1½″ fudge factor. If the hexagons are too large, they become ungainly and pull too much color and design into each block. The aim of this process is to separate the fabric into its individual colors to make "pieces of color."

Cutting Process

You can cut hexagons with either a 60° triangle ruler or a rectangular ruler that features a 60° angle line.

1. From the stacked and pinned fabric, cut 6 strips 3¾″ wide.

☀ *tip* Remember, as you cut a strip that has been pinned, add a pin to the main body of the fabric to maintain the alignment. Pinning this way will hold the uncut piece intact. I have stored pinned fabric for years, and the alignment of the stack remains perfect.

Insert a pin into the remaining fabric.

2. Lay out the 3¾″ strip horizontally, keeping the 6 layers neatly aligned.

60° TRIANGLE RULER

1. Place the ruler close to the selvage with the ruler's 3¾″ mark at one cut edge and the point of the triangle ruler at the other edge.

60° triangle ruler aligned on fabric

2. Cut along one side of the triangle ruler, and then gently position a small rectangular ruler against the triangle. Remove the triangle ruler and make a right-handed cut. (I know there are some people who can cut upside down, but I cannot, so I need a way to keep my cutting to the right.)

Lining up a small ruler

3. For the next cut, place the 60° triangle ruler on the strip so an upside-down triangle in the fabric is skipped. Be sure that the right edge of the ruler is against the right edge of the fabric, the point of the ruler is on the top edge of the fabric strip, and the lower edge of the fabric is along the ruler's 3¾″ mark.

4. Make the right-handed cut, then gently place the small ruler against the triangle ruler. Remove the triangle ruler and make the second cut. In this way, you have cut 2 triangles at the same time.

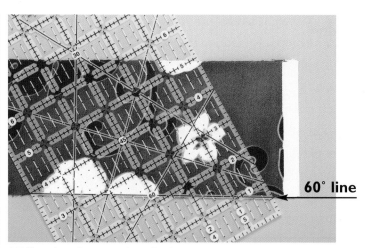
60° line along bottom edge of strip

2. The long edge of the ruler produces the 60° cutting edge. Once you have made that first cut, pivot the ruler to place a 60° line along the top edge of the strip. Cut the triangle. If your ruler has only one 60° line, turn over the ruler to place the line on the top edge.

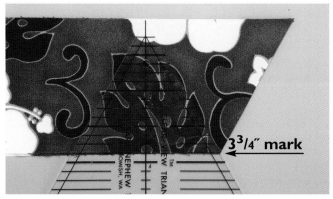
Cut 2 triangles.

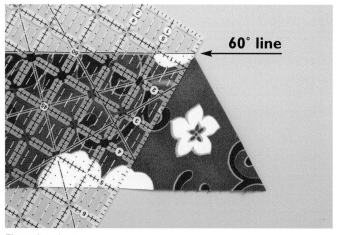
First triangle cut

tip   If you are using a 60° triangle ruler with a blunt tip, place the ruler's 3½″ mark on the edge of the fabric strip. These rulers cut triangles with only a ¼″ seam allowance at the tip. Even though there is no tip on the ruler, make the rotary cutter move as though there were. In this way, the triangle will have the needed point.

RECTANGULAR RULER WITH A 60° LINE

1. Place the ruler's 60° line along the bottom edge of the strip.

3. Continue along the strip, turning the ruler to align the 60° lines on the bottom edge and then the top edge of the strip.

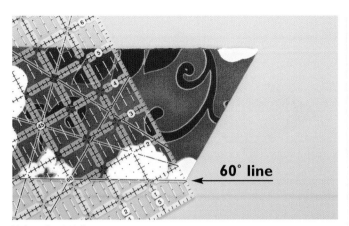

Using the 60° line

Sewing the Hexagons

Because you have cut equilateral triangles, you can assemble the hexagon in 3 different ways with each triangle point in the center of the hexagon.

Whichever method you use, every triangle you cut produces a stack of 6 identical triangles that will form one block. I keep the blocks in order by piling them one stack on the next in different directions as I cut.

Each strip yields 18 or 19 stacks of triangles. This gives you plenty of blocks to play with later. Each strip produces a different array of triangles, possibly even different colors, depending on your fabric.

If the fabric repeats several times from selvage to selvage, be aware that as you cut, you may end up with duplicate triangles. If the triangles begin to repeat, turn the strip around and trim ¼˝ or so from the edge of the strip, following the 60° line. The next triangle will be different from any previously cut.

Trim ¼˝ from strip.

Same triangles, 3 different hexagons

For this process, keep the straight of grain to the outside edge of the block. You can see the straight of grain most easily by looking at the wrong side of the fabric, where it is easier to see the threads that did not get any dye.

2 pairs of triangles and 2 triangles remaining

Straight of grain

2. Press the seams open. This helps distribute the bulk that results when 6 seams come together.

3. Place the 2 sewn pairs of triangles on the table, with the center points facing up. Place a remaining triangle next to each pair so that the straight of grain is along the outside edge. Note that the design on the fabric should be oriented the same way in each triangle.

I don't worry about bias. I think of it as that extra stretch that is sometimes needed to make corners line up with each other. It is easy to recognize the straight of grain so that you always know how to orient the triangles.

Reorganizing triangles so that each hexagon becomes a perfect arrangement takes a great deal of time. Not every hexagon can be the most beautiful. Many times, the most beautiful hexagons just don't seem to fit into the quilt. Some hexagons are good for transition (see page 35 for design ideas). Bear in mind that this is a serendipitous approach—let the designs fall where they may.

Sew the triangles into half hexagons, then pin them together and place them on the design wall. You will sew together the complete hexagons later.

1. Sew 2 triangles together with the straight of grain along the outside edge, sewing with a ¼″ seam from the center to the outside edge. Repeat this process with 2 more triangles. Set aside the remaining 2 triangles.

Placement of third triangle

When this third triangle is lined up, all the points match up. The points are your friends; they help align the third triangle.

Align the third triangle.

4. Sew a third triangle to each sewn pair. Press the seams open.

5. You now have 2 halves of a hexagon. Do *not* sew the hexagon together; rather, pin it together. Instead of pinning as the seam would be sewn, just pin the pieces together, with the edge of half of one hexagon overlapping the edge of its mate. By pinning the hexagon, the block will lie flat when placed on the design wall, and the 2 halves will stay together. You don't want to mix up hexagons.

Pin the hexagon halves together.

Original fabric for *Hiding in the Garden*

Hiding in the Garden: Hexagons and Cubes, 69″ × 63$\frac{1}{2}$″, machine pieced and quilted by the author. I added cubes to this quilt and tried to hide some of them better than others. People are always wondering whether they have found all the cubes.

Designing With Hexagons

Detail of *Chickens in My Yard*

The color and print in the fabric does the design work. The shape of the images on each kaleidoscope comes from the fabric. Shapes change just as they do with each twist of an actual kaleidoscope. For example, leaves on the fabric may have been transformed into curves that fit together and form a flower shape, or simple lines may have been changed to form stars. By using relatively small triangles, the individual colors of the fabric have been separated and disassembled.

DIVIDE THE HEXAGONS INTO COLOR STACKS

Look at each hexagon block to determine its overall color. Make stacks of the different colors that have emerged from your fabric. Keep these colors together to form the palette for your quilt design.

Stacks of colors

You will probably have some blocks that don't fit easily into any stack of color. This will most likely occur when there is an equal amount of two or more colors in a block, so one color is not prominent. As you separate colors, more stacks will begin to emerge. These additional stacks will provide a good transition from one color to the next. Add an extra stack of color wherever it makes sense to you; what started as three stacks might become four or five.

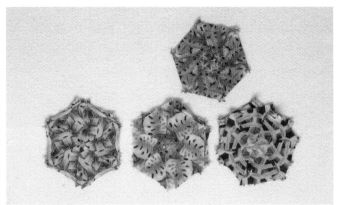

Adding stacks

Separating the stacks by color and density of color is a starting point. Like an artist lays colors on a palette, you are doing the same with the colors in the hexagons.

TO THE DESIGN WALL

Now let's move from paint to painting. It is time to go to the design wall. Hexagons are a very special shape. They form a honeycomb, and they snuggle neatly together with no space between them. This means that all the shapes on the design wall will make up the quilt, with no additional fabric.

Beginning with your favorite stack of color, put all the hexagons from that stack on the design wall.

Place hexagons on the design wall.

Chickens in My Yard, 72˝ × 64˝, machine pieced and quilted by the author. I love chickens. The name was a natural since the fabric featured grass and chickens.

Fabric for *Chickens in My Yard*

A Chicken in Every Pot, 55˝ x 49˝, machine pieced and quilted by the author. Not only are there cubes hiding among the chickens, but a couple of the sides of the cubes are made of snakeskin fabric. No one should be too comfortable, not even chickens on a quilt.

Detail of *A Chicken in Every Pot*

Put your favorite color in the center of the design wall, which is the center of the quilt. These hexagons may not stay there, but it is a good starting place.

Place hexagons on the wall with either the point at the top or a flat edge at the top. It does not matter which orientation you use, but remember to be consistent throughout.

As hexagons are combined, some will be more color intense than others, even though they came from the same stack. These more intense colors belong together. In the photograph, all of one stack was put on the design wall.

All of one stack

The predominantly green hexagons—the most intense color—are in a cluster, and those with the most blue are in another group.

Adding a secondary color

As shown here, hexagons with the most green were kept together on one side and then those with a brown background were added. The brown hexagons became the transition to gold, the next stack of color. Put the next stack of color from your palette on the design wall so you can determine where you are heading in terms of color.

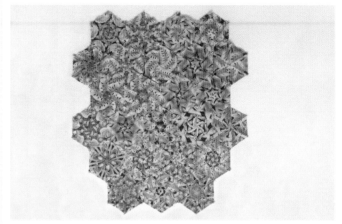

Yet another arrangement

DESIGN CONSIDERATIONS

There are several things to consider when working with kaleidoscope blocks.

Kaleidoscopes are made up of two major design elements—the colors within the hexagon and the shape of the design elements that form the kaleidoscope.

When two or three hexagons with similar design and color are placed next to each other, they will appear to merge. The seam between them disappears, as in the photo.

Seamlessness between hexagons

The shapes at the edges of each hexagon in this photo are so similar that the eye is fooled and a distinct hexagon cannot be easily seen. This effect will not happen with every group of hexagons, but it will happen with some. The more often it happens, the more the quilt will exhibit a watercolor effect.

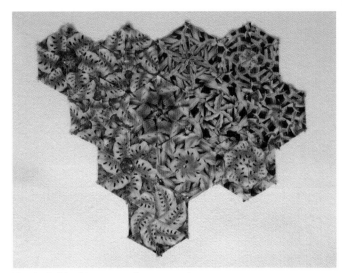

The individual hexagon disappeared.

Where the color and design element at the edge of one block is similar to the next, the transition from hexagon to hexagon will be seamless. For example, there may be a flower or a color that is at the edge of both blocks. The eye easily moves from block to block without a sharp break in color or texture—this effect is what you want to aim for. A successful quilt design creates a surface in which a single hexagon cannot be easily identified. There should be no abrupt changes. The quilt should flow and the eye move over the entire quilt, maybe stopping here and there, but without jarring areas.

It should be noted that in these examples there are large leaves and narrow leaves. The large leaves are placed together, and the small leaves are placed together. This separation is not an accident. The small leaves would look strange next to the large ones; they only mix well when the hexagons have a combination of the two leaf shapes and when the transition is made from one to the next. This is the transition of shape. It is less obvious than color, but it is just as important.

CRITIQUE YOUR DESIGN

As you add blocks to the design wall, step back and review. If a hexagon is in the wrong place, it will stand out. You will not see that even flow from one block to the next.

The hexagon that pops out in this example has too much gold and not enough blue to blend with the hexagons next to it. It belongs with hexagons of more similar color and design elements.

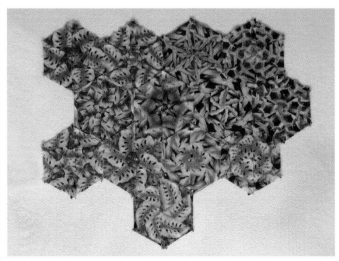

One misplaced hexagon

Maid in Japan, 86˝ x 56˝, machine pieced and quilted by Joy Pelzmann. Since many of the blocks were the same, Joy separated them into three panels within the quilt.

Detail of *Maid in Japan*

In the following examples, the same hexagons are arranged in two different ways. In Design 1, the gold is to the left. In Design 2, the gold is to the right. The possibilities are endless. Find the one that is most appealing. It is almost impossible to use every hexagon. There always seem to be a few that just don't fit anywhere. These are often the hexagons that seemed to be the most beautiful or those with the most background.

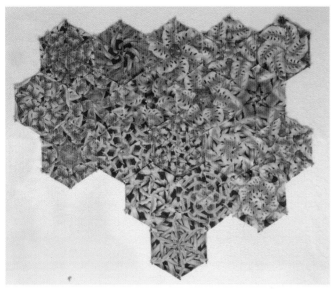

Design 1

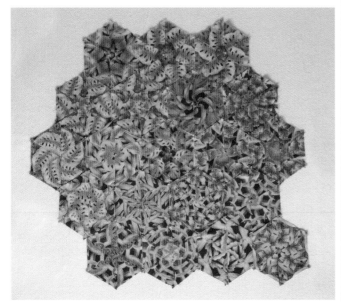

Design 2

Several of the quilts shown here contain contrasting patchwork cubes among the hexagons. This block design was developed by Sara Nephew. I use these cube blocks to add interest to the quilt.

Another fun variation is adding a whole hexagon cut from the original fabric. Can you find the cowboys in my quilt *Cowboys*? There is even one triangle cut from the red border fabric. This indicates how many mistakes you can get away with on these one-block wonders!

Detail of *Cowboys*

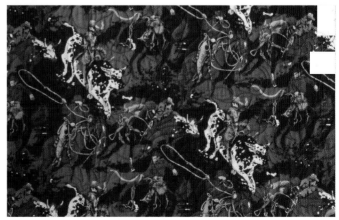

Fabric for *Cowboys*

Cowboys, 57″ × 72″, machine pieced and quilted by the author. This is one of my favorite quilts because I mixed in whole hexagons of the original fabric, and it is hard to find these. This really portrays how we can train the eye to see kaleidoscopes, even when they are not there.

Shape and Size of the Final Quilt

Keep in mind the ultimate shape and size of the quilt you are making. Is it to be as close to a square as you can get, or do you want it more rectangular? If it is rectangular, will it be long or wide? I like to make quilts that are wider than they are long. Think about the final shape and size as you decide how many hexagons you want in a row and how many rows there should be. There is no right way to arrange these hexagons—just your way.

When all of the hexagons are arranged on the wall, it will look like it has ragged edges. You can straighten two sides of the quilt by either adding or removing half hexagons.

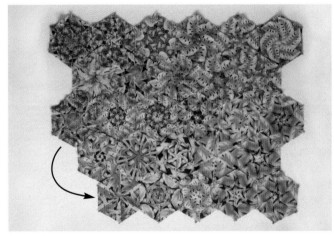

Ragged edges

Add or remove half hexagons.

Sometimes a half hexagon that you removed from one side of the quilt can be added to the space on the other side of the quilt. You will also have extra hexagons that you can divide into halves and use to even up the edges.

For now, leave the other sides ragged. These sides are discussed later when you finish the quilt (see page 41). Let the quilt simmer on the design wall for several days before even considering sewing it together. Look at it in both daylight and artificial light. Invite your family to express their opinions. Let them move some of the blocks around. Whatever you do, have fun.

Sewing the Quilt Top Together

You now have half hexagons that are pinned together to form the whole quilt top. As you place the half hexagons on the design wall, rows will become apparent. From the top is the right half of one hexagon, then the left half of the next one and on down the row or across, depending on how you placed the hexagons on the wall.

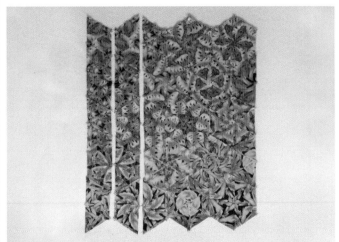

Rows of half hexagons

1. To begin a row, first remove the pins that are holding the halves of each hexagon together.

2. As you take each half hexagon off the wall, pin it to the next half in the row. Do not mix up the order, or they will never go back together again. Put a pin in the end hexagon to orient this row so you can correctly place it on the wall after you have sewn and ironed it.

> ☀ *tip* If you take 2 rows to the sewing machine at a time, put 2 orientation pins into the second row so you can distinguish it from the first.

3. When you sew the half hexagons together, the points on the triangles will line up. Use these points to align the seams so they meet exactly.

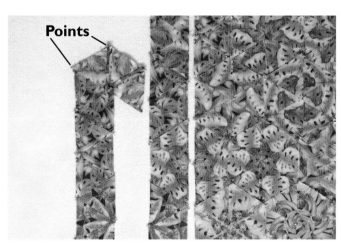

Lining up the points

4. Press all seams open.

5. Place the rows back on the wall in their original places.

6. Sew the rows together. As you take the rows off the wall, put an orientation pin in one end. This way, after you sew and press them, you can place them on the wall in the correct position. When you place the rows right sides together, the points neatly fit one on top of the other. This aligns all the seams. Keep in mind that these hexagons have bias edges, which offer a little extra stretch that may help line up the points exactly if necessary.

Align the rows.

7. Press the seams open to distribute the bulk.

This is a very user-friendly process. If the centers of the hexagons aren't exact, don't worry. There is so much activity, so much for the eye to focus on, that mistakes are hard to find.

FINISHING THE EDGES

After you sew all the rows, you still have two ragged sides. If you placed the hexagon blocks to form vertical rows, the ragged edges will be at the top and bottom. If you arranged the blocks in horizontal rows, the ragged edges will be on the sides. You have several options for dealing with these ragged edges.

Ragged edges

Trim the ragged edge.

One option is to trim the ragged edges by placing a ruler along the inside edge of the points. Line up the inside edges and cut. Once you attach a border, the edges will look very natural. The eye always wants to complete the design. With so many intact hexagons, the eye has learned what they should look like and is fooled into believing that they all look that way. Study the quilts in this book. If I hadn't just told you that a whole side of hexagons was cut short, would you have noticed?

Instead of cutting off the ragged points, another option is to sew half triangles of the fabric of the first border to the ends of each row before sewing the rows together. This will make the quilt appear to float on the border. The pattern for this half triangle (see page 70) is slightly oversized. Cut the total number needed, reversing half. Center the triangles on the sides of the hexagons. After joining the rows, trim the triangles to form a straight edge.

Floating quilt

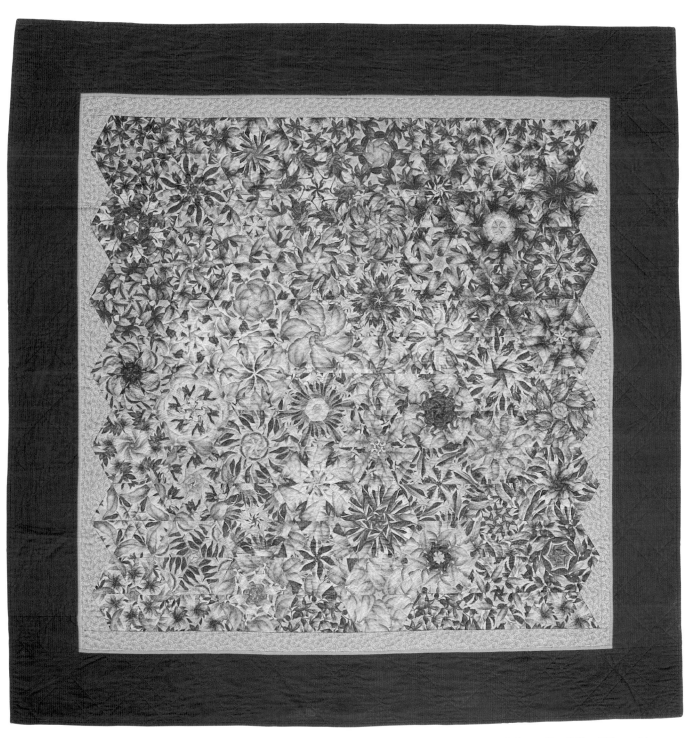

Autumn Day, 55″ × 56″, machine pieced and quilted by the author. I added half triangles of the first border fabric to the sides of the hexagons to float the quilt.

Detail of *Autumn Day*

Finished size: 72˝ × 60˝

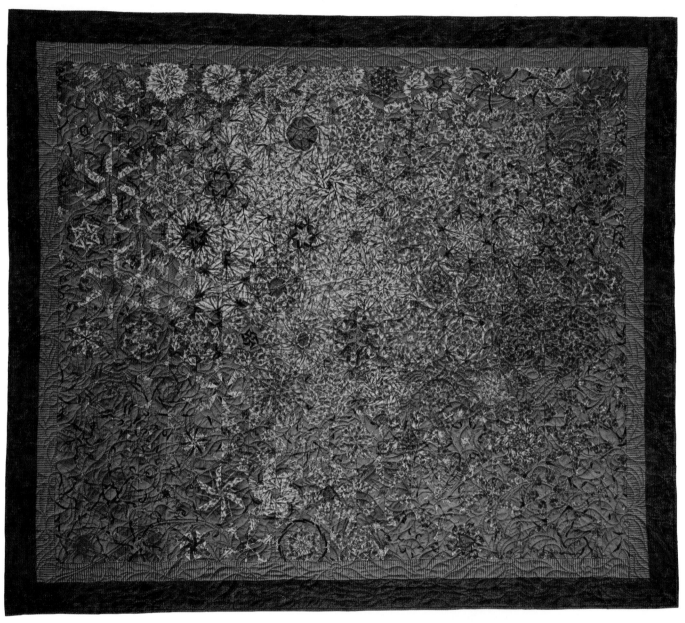

Subtle Red, machine pieced and quilted
by the author.

Detail of *Subtle Red*

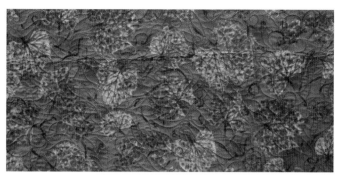

Fabric for *Subtle Red*

This is a great quilt to snuggle under while watching TV or reading a book.

A fabric with a 24˝ repeat will produce a good lap-sized quilt. I chose a fabric with very little color change. This choice was my attempt at subtlety, and red is my favorite color. Although this fabric has a fair amount of background, the background is not plain—it has a ribbon running though it. So, there are two design elements: the ribbon and the flowers.

Materials

- 4¾ yards fabric for blocks
- ½ yard matching fabric for inner borders
- ¾ yard coordinating fabric for outer borders
- 3½ yards fabric for backing
- ½ yard for binding
- Batting: 76˝ × 64˝

Before you begin, refer to pages 19–22 for cutting, layering, and pinning repeats. Then reread pages 27–31 for cutting and sewing hexagon blocks. Refer to pages 63–64 for measuring and cutting borders.

Cutting

Block fabric:

Cut 6 repeats. Layer, align, and pin. Trim one edge. Cut 6 strips 3¾˝ × the width of the fabric. From the strips, cut 108–114 stacks of 60° triangles.

Matching fabric:

For the inner borders, cut 6 strips 2¼˝ × the width of the fabric.

Coordinating fabric:

For the outer borders, cut 7 strips 3¼˝ × the width of the fabric.

Binding fabric:

Cut 7 strips 2˝ × the width of the fabric.

Sewing

1. Sew the triangles into pairs of half hexagons. Pin the pairs together to make hexagon blocks.

2. Arrange the blocks on the design wall, with pointed edges vertical, in 10 rows of 10 blocks each. Refer to pages 32–38 for ideas on how to arrange the blocks.

3. Divide the remaining blocks into halves. Arrange them along either side to fill in the blanks and to create straight sides. You will have extra blocks.

4. Sew the hexagons together in vertical rows. Join the rows (see pages 40–41).

5. Cut the points off the blocks on the top and the bottom of the quilt top to form straight edges (see page 42).

Finishing

1. Sew the 2¼˝ inner border strips into 1 long strip. Cut 2 pieces 63½˝ and sew to the top and bottom. Cut 2 pieces 55˝ and sew to the sides of the quilt.

2. Sew the 3¼˝ outer border strips into 1 long strip. Cut 2 pieces 67˝ and sew to the top and bottom. Cut 2 pieces 60½˝ and sew to the sides of the quilt.

3. Quilt and bind.

Octagon Blocks

Blue on Blue, 49″ × 37″, machine pieced
and quilted by the author. The original fabric
is in the border.

Because the triangles for octagons use a relatively narrow slice of fabric, each block creates a pattern that is very different from the original fabric. When the octagons are coupled with squares, they fill the entire surface with pattern and color in a way that no other process can. Each block is new and different, with energy all its own. Ironing has never been my favorite task, but ironing a completed block and seeing it look so completely different from the previous block is reward in itself. Octagons can be any size, but for this process, only one size is used.

Cutting Process

1. You will use a template as a guideline to cut the triangles from the pinned and stacked strips of fabric. Trace the pattern (see page 70) onto a piece of template plastic. The parallelogram shape measures 4˝ across in one direction and 3⅛˝ across in the other direction. Carefully cut out the template plastic pattern.

2. From the stacked and pinned fabric, cut 4 strips 4˝ wide.

For every 2 strips used to make octagons, cut 1 strip 2¾˝ wide to be used later for the Sensational Squares (see page 56).

⁂ tip Remember, as you cut a strip that has been pinned, add a pin to the main body of the fabric to maintain the alignment.

3. Place the template on the 4˝ strip, beginning at the right edge of the fabric. Place a small ruler to the left of the template and *gently* move it so it rests against the template.

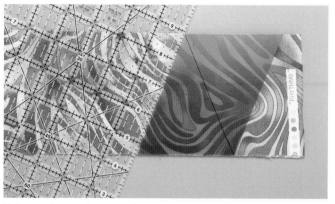

Ruler resting against template

4. Once the small ruler is against the template, carefully remove the template and cut along the ruler.

⁂ tip Do not use the template as the edge to cut against. It is much too easy to cut the template and destroy the nice clean edge you worked so hard to create.

5. Turn the newly cut piece 180°. Again, align the template against the cut edge of the fabric, and gently move a small ruler against the template. Remove the template and cut along the edge of the ruler.

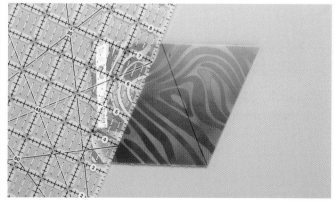

Cut along edge of ruler.

Detail of *Blue on Blue*

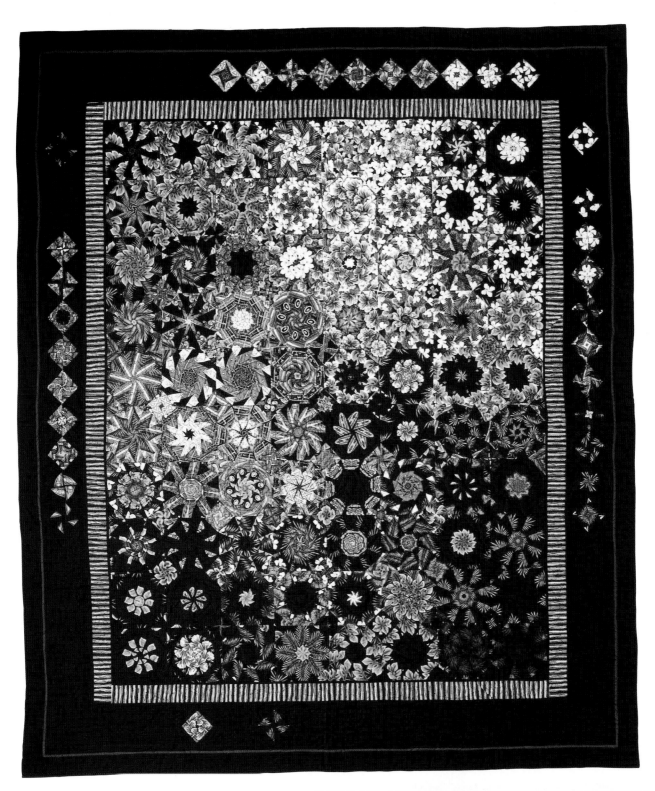

Hawaiian Vacation, 67″ × 79″, machine pieced and quilted by the author. My friend went to Hawaii for a vacation and brought me back the best gift: fabric!

Fabric for *Hawaiian Vacation*

6. While keeping the 8 layers neatly aligned, place a small ruler on the parallelogram from one wide angle to the other wide angle. Cut the parallelogram into 2 isosceles triangles. The narrow angle becomes the center of the octagon.

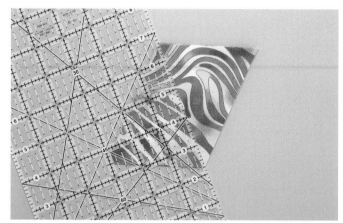

Cut the parallelogram.

7. Continue cutting the rest of the strip into parallelograms. Cut each into 2 stacks of triangles. Each stack forms 1 octagon.

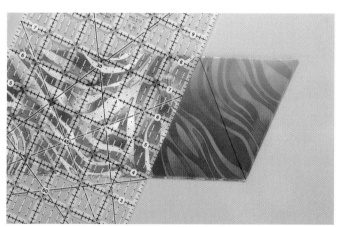

Cut the rest of the strip.

☀ *tip* Sometimes the width of the fabric will yield all but the tip of the last parallelogram. Cut the last parallelogram, and then cut from one wide angle to the other to make just one more stack of triangles. Discard the stack of incomplete triangles.

Sewing the Octagons

Each octagon is a set of 8 triangles. You need to keep the pieces of each octagon together throughout the sewing process. Take care not to sew triangles from one octagon onto another.

1. The narrow point of the triangle is the center of the octagon. Using a ¼" seam, sew 2 triangles together from the center to the outside edge. The center *must* match; any discrepancies between the triangles will be hidden in the outer seam allowance.

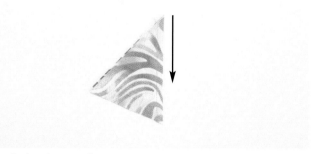

Sew 2 triangles together.

2. Sew 3 more pairs of triangles together for each octagon.

3. Press all seams open. You now have 4 quarter octagons. Do not cut off the little points. They will help you align the next pieces.

4. Sew a quarter octagon to another quarter octagon, lining up the points at the top and bottom. You now have a half octagon.

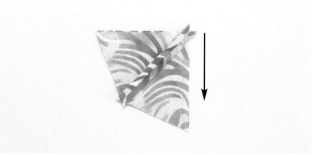

Line up 2 quarter octagons.

5. Repeat Step 4 with the remaining 2 quarter octagons. Press the seams open.

6. Sew the octagon halves together, lining up the points at the top, bottom, and center.

Line up half octagons.

> ✶ *tip* Be sure this final seam is straight. A curve in this last seam will yield a block that pokes up like a little hat or a block with a rippled edge.

Seam curved in

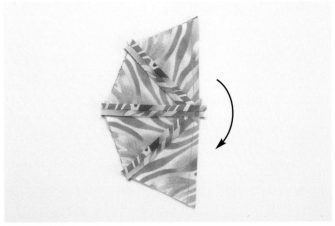

Seam curved out

Straight seam

7. Press this center seam open. Pressing the seams open not only eliminates the bulk at the center, it also avoids a ridge that can form when all the seam allowances are on one side.

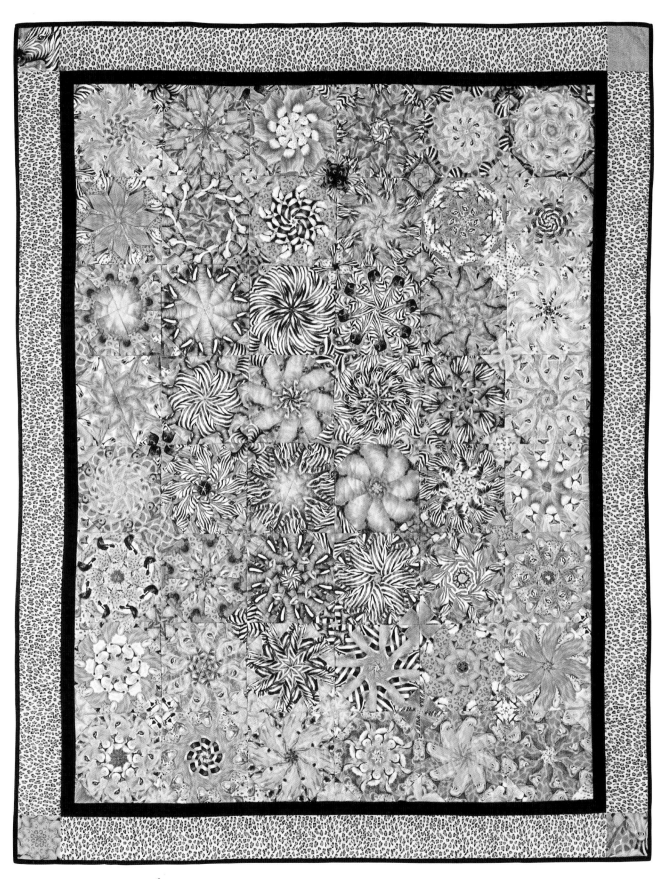

The Plains of Africa, 44″ × 56$\frac{1}{2}$″,
machine pieced and quilted by the author.

Night Sky in Sedona, 64″ × 75″, machine
pieced by Meg Devine, quilted by the author.

Designing With Octagons

At this point, there is no design planned for the quilt top. While making the octagons, it is great fun to admire the blocks as you press them and randomly place them on your design wall. Because each triangle is narrow, the octagons are very different from each other.

DIVIDE THE OCTAGONS INTO COLOR STACKS

The color of each kaleidoscope is determined by the location in the fabric where the cuts were originally made. Arrange the octagons into stacks of colors. When a block does not fit into any one stack, it is time to begin a new one. There is no rule about how many stacks to make: sort the octagons into as many piles as necessary. Keep in mind that there are both color and intensity of color—although two kaleidoscopes may be the same color, one may appear darker than the other. You will probably divide these into two stacks. The stacks become your palette—just as a painter applies paints to his palette, so too are you arranging octagons into colors.

In the example of the zebra fabric used in *Zebras* (page 6), though the color doesn't change, the density of the stripes makes some blocks appear darker than others. It is interesting to note that some colors that were barely noticeable in the original fabric are much more obvious when used in a kaleidoscope. I saw the original zebra fabric as basically one color and was surprised at how light or dark the different octagons were.

TO THE DESIGN WALL

When all the octagons are in stacks, it is time to move to the design wall. A blank wall … stacks of octagons … where to begin? Start with your favorite color stack. The middle of a quilt is usually the focal point, so begin by putting your favorite color in the center of the quilt. It may not stay there, but it is a good starting place. I don't want my favorite color off in some corner; I want it right where I can see it. Begin by putting the entire stack on the wall, before arranging the octagons side by side. It is helpful to see all of your choices before making final decisions.

Stacks of octagons

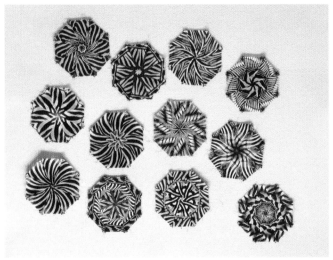

Octagons on the design wall

The aim is to make a smooth transition from one octagon to the next. This is done both by color and by design within the octagons. Even though the color might be right, the design of one octagon may not match the one next to it. When the eye can follow a pattern from one octagon to the next, the seam between them disappears.

Poor choice of neighbors

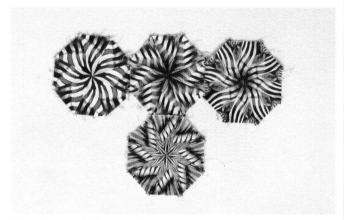

Seamlessness between octagons

CRITIQUE YOUR DESIGN

Step back to see where the seam between octagons disappears and where it does not. When the transition from one color to the next works well, the eye moves comfortably around the quilt. The center block in the next-to-bottom row does not blend into the others around it.

You will notice that when four octagons are put together, there is a diamond-shaped space between them. You will fill these spaces with Sensational Squares (page 56)—stay tuned for more information.

Open diamond space

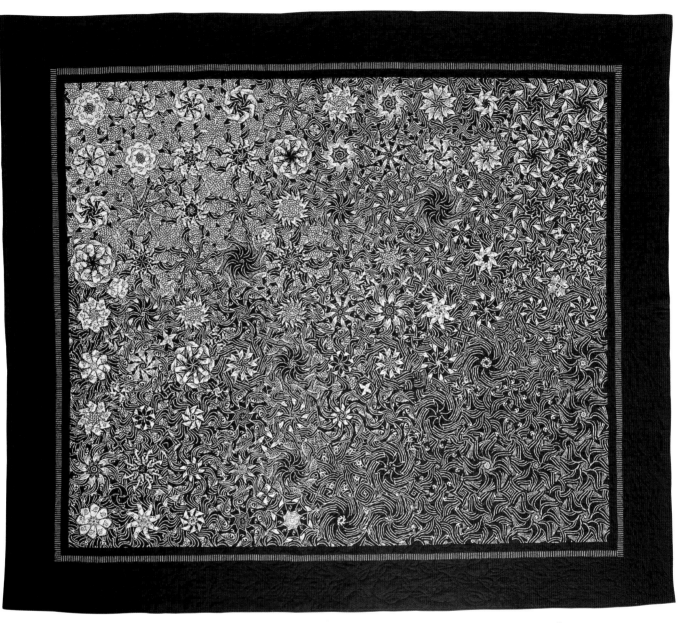

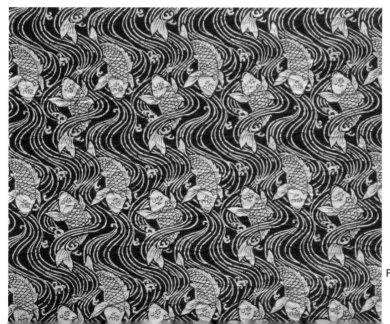

Japanese Fish, 67$\frac{1}{2}$″ × 77″, machine pieced and quilted by the author. This was such simple fabric and yet it produced such variety that it is even hard to see the fish. I found that I liked the design of the lines better anyway.

Fabric for *Japanese Fish*

Shape and Size of the Final Quilt

Begin in the center or in a corner. Begin with the stack you like the most. The colors that are the most similar belong together. Keep in mind the shape of your final quilt. A 24″ repeat of 5⅓ yards of fabric produces more than 90 octagons.

BLOCK ARRANGEMENT

- For a square quilt, arrange the blocks 9 octagons by 9 octagons.

- For a nearly square quilt, arrange the blocks 9 octagons by 10 octagons.

- For a long and narrow quilt, arrange the blocks 8 octagons by 11 octagons.

There is no rule here. The size and the shape of the quilt are up to you.

Keep moving the octagons around until you find a pleasing combination. Stand back. Come back later. View this in different lighting: daylight, incandescent light, twilight. Let your family give opinions, and let them move the octagons around. When you find a combination you like, live with it for a couple of days. When you are satisfied, it is time to add the squares.

Sensational Squares

There is no other term for these squares but sensational! They are magic. They make me giggle. How can something so easy to cut produce something with so much variety and interest?

1. Cut 2¾″ × 2¾″ squares from the 2¾″ strips.

2¾″ squares

2. Work with each stack of squares separately. Without getting the stack out of alignment, divide it into 2 stacks of 4 layers each. Set them side by side on the cutting table so they face the same way. Cut 1 stack diagonally from lower left to upper right; cut the other stack diagonally from upper left to lower right.

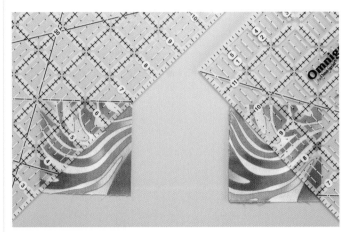

Cut squares into triangles.

This technique gives you the most variety. Each stack of 4 half-square triangles will make 1 kaleidoscopic square. The 90° angle is the center of the square, which when turned is a diamond or a square on point.

Kaleidoscopic square

3. These squares will fit into the space between 4 octagons. When a square is correctly placed between 4 octagons, the square will disappear.

Correct placement of squares

When you step back from the design wall, the square will appear to be gone. The 4 octagons are now blended together, like clay being smoothed out. As with all designing, be aware of the color and design elements in each square. Place a square between octagons of similar color. When the coloration is correct, elements of the pattern merge. If this blending does not happen, move the square to another place or look for another square to fit into that space.

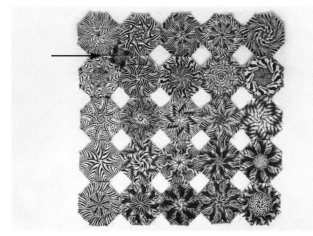

Incorrect placement of square

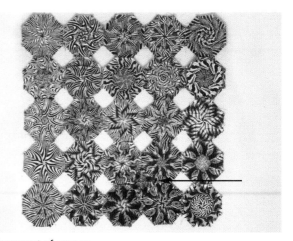

Better placement of square

Take your time!

I remember putting the first Sensational Square on the design wall. When I stepped back, I couldn't find it. I had to remind myself that there was only one square among all the octagons, and yet I could not find it.

Use half squares (2 triangles) to fill the spaces at the edges of the quilt and quarter squares (1 triangle) to finish the corners.

Half squares for the sides

Finishing corners

When all the squares are placed on the quilt, the result is a whole cloth that has more intensity and interest than the original fabric. It is exciting to stand back and look at this final arrangement on the wall.

Final placement

You'll cut many more squares than you'll need. This provides the flexibility to choose just the right square to fit any space. You'll have many squares left over, but this is a small price to pay for the perfectly placed square. You can use these extras in the border or piece them into the backing.

Leave this completely designed quilt on the design wall for a couple of days to see it in different kinds of lighting, to live with it, and to make minor changes.

Sewing the Quilt Top Together

Now that the octagon quilt is on the design wall exactly the way you want it, it is time to sew it together.

Work on *no more than* 2 blocks at a time. More than that is confusing, and you do not want to lose the placement of these pieces after you worked so hard to get it just the way you want it.

1. While all the octagons are still on the wall, choose one to work with. It is best to start with a corner octagon. Pin a triangle to each corner of that octagon.

Pin corners to an octagon.

2. The 4 corners come from 4 different Sensational Squares that surround this octagon. Before removing this octagon from the wall, place a pin at the top of the octagon in such a way that the pin will not interfere with your sewing or ironing. This pin will always point you to the top of the block, allowing you to place it back on the design wall in the exact original position. This way, each triangle will line up again to its Sensational Square.

Orientation pin

> ※ *tip* It may be helpful to use a flower pin as the orientation pin—just be careful not to iron it. If you are working on 2 octagons at a time, put 2 orientation pins on the second octagon so you know the difference between the first and second when it is time to put them back on the design wall.

2 octagons with orientation pins

3. It is OK that the half-square triangles are a little large for the sides of the octagon. Attach each triangle so the corners that extend beyond each end are about equal and the 90° angle points to the center of the octagon. Sew with a ¼″ seam.

Placement of corners

4. Press the seams open. Do not remove the orientation pin. Go back to the cutting table and square the block to a 6½″ × 6½″ square.

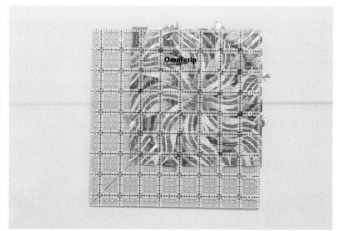

Square the block.

Do not worry about the corners not being the same as on the next block. There is so much pattern and movement that it does not matter. When I started making these, I used to cut the corners so they lined up to the remaining edges of the octagon, with no attention paid to the size of square that this became. Squaring up is as close to perfect as I get.

5. Put the block back on the wall in position. When all the triangles are sewn to the octagons, the blocks become squares. Sew the squares together in rows and join the rows to make a quilt. Once the octagons become squares, sewing them together is no different from sewing any other quilt that has square blocks.

6. Iron all seams open to distribute the bulk. This step is not necessary, but if seams are ironed to one side, a ridge will form at every line because there is so much fabric.

You now have your quilt top finished. All you need are borders.

Finished size: 77½″ × 71½″

High Fiber Diet, machine pieced
and quilted by the author.

What else can you say about fabric with fruits and vegetables except high fiber? This quilt shows less transition between blocks than others—I love it when the fabric disappears. However, the print created fun and unexpected kaleidoscope designs.

Materials

- 5¾ yards fabric for blocks
- 1 yard contrasting fabric for inner and outer borders
- 1½ yards coordinating fabric for middle borders
- 4¼ yards for backing
- ⅝ yard for binding
- Batting: 82″ × 76″

Before you begin, refer to pages 19–22 for cutting, layering, and pinning repeats. Then reread pages 47–50 for cutting and sewing octagon blocks. Refer to pages 63–64 for measuring and cutting borders.

Cutting

Block fabric:

Cut 8 repeats. Layer, align and pin. Trim one edge.

Cut 4 strips 4″ × the width of the fabric. From the strips, cut 90 stacks of triangles.

From the leftover ends of the strips, cut 3 stacks of 4″ triangles to make large Sensational Squares for the borders.

Cut 2 strips 2¾″ × the remaining width of the fabric. Cut into 2¾″ × 2¾″ squares, then triangles for Sensational Squares.

Contrasting fabric:

For the inner borders, cut 6 strips 2″ × the width of the fabric.

For the outer borders, cut 8 strips 2¼″ × the width of the fabric.

Coordinating fabric:

Cut 7 strips 6″ × the width of the fabric.

Binding fabric:

Cut 8 strips 2″ × the width of the fabric.

Sewing

1. Sew the triangles into 90 octagons.

2. Arrange the octagons on the design wall in rows, with 10 blocks across and 9 blocks down.

3. Place the 2¾″ triangles into Sensational Squares and arrange them between the blocks and on the sides and corners (see page 56).

4. Sew the triangles to the octagons.

5. Press and square the blocks to 6½″ × 6½″.

6. Sew the blocks into rows. Join the rows.

Finishing

1. Sew the 2″ inner border strips into 1 long strip. Cut 2 pieces 60½″ and sew to the top and bottom of the quilt. Cut 2 pieces 57½″ and sew to the sides of the quilt.

2. Sew the triangles cut from the leftover fabric into Sensational Squares. Border the squares with 1½″ strips cut from scraps of the contrasting fabric. Trim the blocks to 6″.

3. Sew the 6″ middle border strips together into one long strip. Cut 2 pieces 57½″ and sew to the sides of the quilt. Cut 1 piece 69″. Add a 6″ Sensational Square to one end and sew to the top of the quilt. Cut 1 piece 63½″. Add the remaining 6″ Sensational Squares to the ends and sew to the bottom of the quilt.

4. Sew the 2¼″ outer border strips into 1 long strip. Cut 2 pieces 74½″ and sew to the top and bottom of the quilt. Cut 2 pieces 72″ and sew to the sides of the quilt.

5. Quilt and bind.

Borders

Red, 64″ × 78″, machine pieced and quilted by the author.

Fabric for *Red*

It is fun to add the original fabric as a border, because it is hard to believe that all this variety came from just one fabric. Other fabrics in contrasting or coordinating colors also work well as frames for these one-block wonders. Each color that is added in a border will pull the eye to that color in the quilt, even if it is just a thin line.

Border Variations

Make borders more interesting with patchwork accents. I used extra blocks in the corners of the borders in *Blue on Blue* (page 46). The smaller hexagons in the borders in *Red* were made from triangles cut from a stack of strips that measured 2¾″ instead of 3¾″ wide.

Put those extra Sensational Squares to good use in the borders. Extra squares were pieced into the borders in *Kaleioflower* (page 65) and were set on point in *Hawaiian Vacation* (page 48). I combined patterns in *Hot Chilies* (page 18), using hexagon blocks in the quilt and Sensational Squares in the borders.

Measure the Quilt Top

No matter how much I try, my quilts are never perfectly straight. I use the border fabric to make the quilt perfectly even.

Measure the center width of your quilt. This is the quilt's exact width. Some people measure the center, the top, and the bottom of the quilt and then take an average of the three. I just measure in the center, because that is the size I want the quilt to be. I don't want an average; I want an absolute.

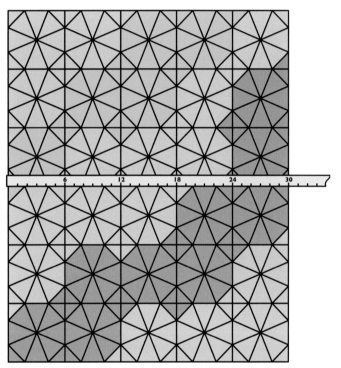
Measure across the center.

WIDTH

1. Cut border strips across the width of the fabric. Sew the strips into 1 long strip. Cut 2 pieces of border fabric exactly the measurement of the width of the quilt.

2. Mark both the center of 1 border piece and the center of the quilt edge.

3. Pin the center of the border to the center of the quilt edge. Pin the ends of the border to the corners of the quilt. Distribute any fullness between the pins.

4. Sew the border piece to the quilt, and press to the border. Repeat for the other side.

LENGTH

1. Measure the length of the quilt through the center of the quilt. Notice that this measurement includes the borders that were just sewn on.

Measure the length of the quilt.

2. Use this measurement to cut the length of the border strips. Pin on the borders and distribute any fullness, as you did for the width borders.

3. Sew and press. Your quilt will now be a perfect rectangle.

Add as many borders as you like. Remember to measure each time to get the exact size of the border being added. The width of the border(s) is your choice. Borders are not only a finishing edge, they can also be used to add a slice of color to the quilt or even as a means to get to the size quilt you desire.

Narrow Accent Borders

Use a narrow border to pull out a color from the body of the quilt. The red border in *Hiding in the Garden: Hexagons and Cubes* (page 31) and the bright green border in *Autumn Day* (page 43) emphasize those colors in the quilts. This is a very quick, easy way to sew an exact ¼″ inner border. I love this technique because it is so easy and looks so hard.

1. Cut the strips ¾″ wide.

2. Sew the border strips to the quilt as you normally would. Iron toward this wee little border.

3. Instead of placing the next border on top to sew, turn the quilt over so the next border is on the bottom. With the narrow border on top, place the presser foot against the last row of stitches, where you added this ¾″ strip. The seam allowance of this border forms a wall against which the presser foot can ride. The width of the foot is ¼″, making it easy to sew a precise, straight seam. You don't even have to pay much attention; it happens by itself!

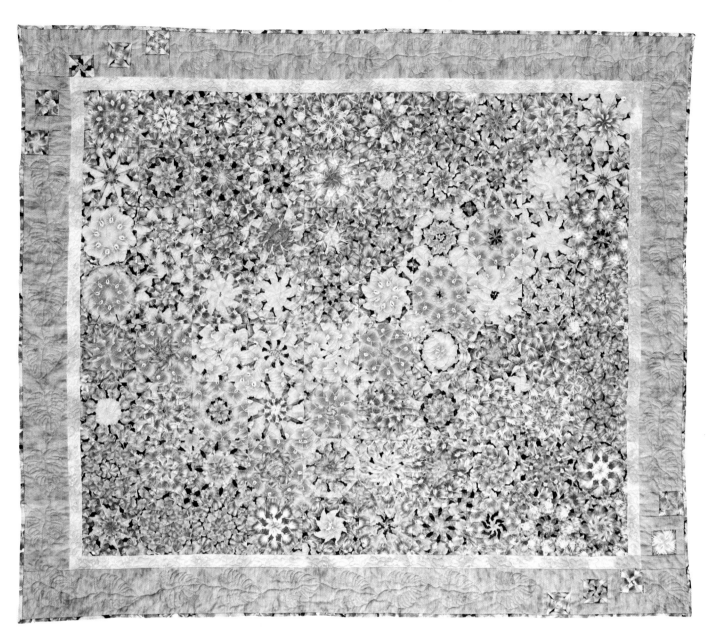

Kaleioflower, 70″ × 62″,
machine pieced and quilted
by Cindy Wilson.

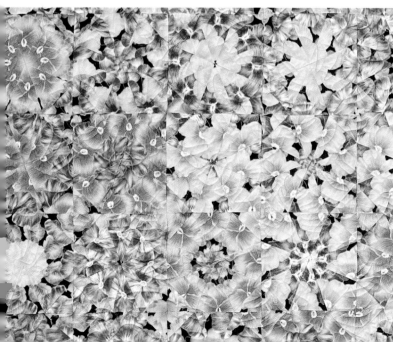

Detail of *Kaleioflower*

What to Do With Extra Kaleidoscopes

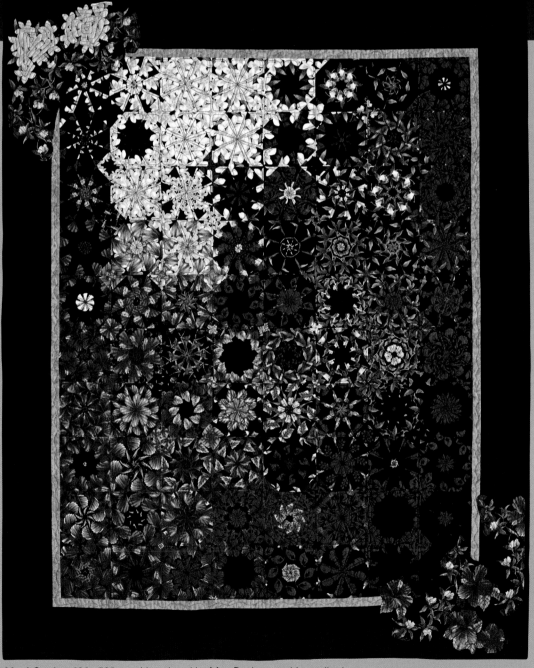

Maui Garden, 63″× 76″, machine pieced by Meg Devine, machine quilted by Runs With Scissors. Meg appliquéd flowers cut from the print to cover some blocks she did not like and they became a wonderful accent.

There always seem to be extra blocks when a quilt top is finished. Often these leftover blocks are the very kaleidoscopes that were thought to be the most beautiful. Don't throw these away; instead, make them into smaller projects such as place mats, table runners, or pot holders.

If your leftovers are octagons, they are already whole. If your leftovers are hexagons, sew the halves together so that you have whole hexagons.

Table Runner With Octagon Kaleidoscopes

Finished size: 18″ × 42″

Zebras on the Run, machine pieced and quilted by the author. It was hard to believe that zebras come in different colors. I thought they were all black and white, but some had more tan than others.

Detail of *Zebras on the Run*

Use leftover blocks from a larger quilt. If you aren't ready to commit to a full quilt, this is a great small starter project. It also makes a great gift!

Materials

- 12 octagon kaleidoscopes
- 12 Sensational Squares
- ³⁄₈ yard dark fabric for inner and outer borders
- ¹⁄₈ yard light fabric for middle border
- ³⁄₄ yard for backing
- ¹⁄₃ yard for binding
- Batting: 22″ × 46″

Cutting

Dark fabric:

For inner borders, cut 3 strips 1″ × the width of the fabric.

For outer borders, cut 3 strips 2³⁄₄″ × the width of the fabric.

Light fabric:

For the middle border, cut 3 strips ³⁄₄″ × the width of the fabric.

Binding:

Cut 4 strips 2″ × the width of the fabric.

Sewing

1. Choose 12 similar octagons.

2. Arrange the octagons on the design wall, 2 across and 6 down.

3. Place Sensational Squares in the spaces between the octagons and in the corners and sides of the table runner.

4. Sew each octagon into a square, using 1 triangle from each of the adjacent Sensational Squares. Remember to place an orientation pin (page 58) in the octagon so you can place it back on the wall in its assigned location. Square blocks to 6½˝.

5. Sew the squares together to form rows, and then join the rows.

Finishing

1. From the 1˝ inner border strips, cut 2 pieces 36½˝ and sew to the sides of the runner. Cut 2 pieces 13½˝ and sew to the ends of the runner.

2. From the ¾˝ middle border strips, cut 2 pieces 37½˝ and sew to the sides of the runner. Cut 2 pieces 14˝ and sew to the ends of the runner. (Refer to page 64 for tips on sewing narrow borders.)

3. From the 2¾˝ outer border strips, cut 2 pieces 38˝ and sew to the sides of the runner. Cut 2 pieces 18½˝ and sew to the ends of the runner.

4. Quilt and bind.

Pot Holders

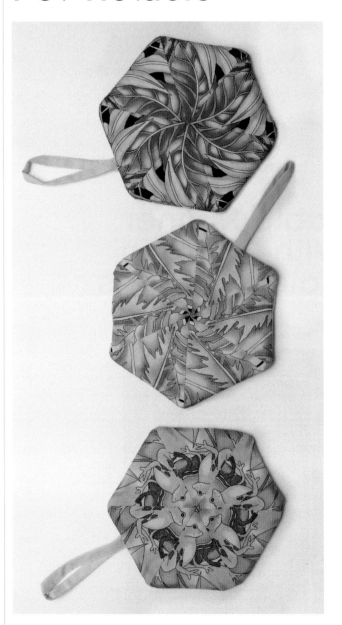

Turn leftover blocks into absolutely wonderful pot holders. Use them yourself, to match your kitchen to your quilt, or give them as gifts. Use a plain backing, something left over from the border fabric, or just something that coordinates with the kaleidoscopes. I use two layers of cotton batting so that heat will not transfer to the hand when used.

Materials

- 3 leftover hexagon or octagon blocks
- ¼ yard for backing
- 9″ × 42″ piece of cotton batting

Cutting

Backing fabric:

For backing, cut 1 piece 8″ × 21″.

For tab loops, cut 3 pieces 1½″ × 8″.

Batting:

Cut 2 pieces 9″ × 21″.

Sewing

1. Make tab loops so the pot holders can hang on a hook. Press the 1½″ fabric pieces in half along the length of the loops. Press again so the long cut edges meet at the fold. Sew along this double fold to hold it in place.

2. Fold each piece in half and pin the raw edges to the center of a straight edge of a leftover hexagon or octagon. Pin to the right side of the block with the loop of the tab toward the center.

3. Layer the pieces of batting and place them on your work surface. Place the backing right side up on the batting. Place the blocks on the batting in a row, right side down. Pin in place.

Layers for pot holder

4. Sew around the blocks, ¼″ from the edge, leaving an opening on one side so that you can turn the pot holder right side out.

Sewn pot holder

5. Cut around the blocks through all the layers. Turn right side out and press. Close the opening with a whip stitch.

6. Quilt in-the-ditch of the seams of the blocks so the pot holders can be washed without losing their shape.

I hope you have enjoyed learning this new process. That is all it is, a process. I know you will never walk into a fabric store and look at fabric the same way. From now on, you will see a piece of fabric and wonder about its possibilities. No more buying fat quarters—now it will be 4½ yards or nothing. Just remember that the fabric, not you, controls what is produced—so sit back, relax, and *have fun.*

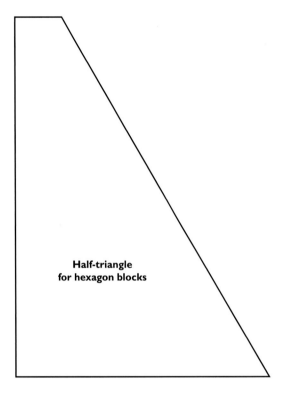

**Half-triangle
for hexagon blocks**

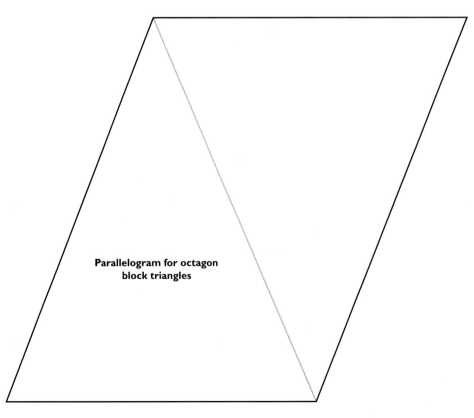

**Parallelogram for octagon
block triangles**

Template Patterns

Maxine Rosenthal started quilting about fifteen years ago. She used to make clothing, but never anything as large or as time-consuming as a quilt. She started with small quilts, miniature ones sewn by hand. She was pretty excited about what she was making, so she hung them on the wall. One summer, her husband's aunt came for a visit; as Maxine sat sewing a miniature quilt, her aunt asked what she was doing. With great pride Maxine said she was making a quilt. Her aunt wanted to know if it was a "knee quilt," because something that size would only be good for the knee; it certainly wouldn't be large enough to keep a whole body warm. Since then, Maxine's quilts have gotten larger, and her walls seem to have gotten smaller, so the quilts are now destined for the bed or the lap.

Maxine did many things before quilting. She had a career writing computer software, and even took a break from that to learn furniture refinishing, which she considered a walk through history. She was commissioned to make a quilt for the movie *Grumpier Old Men*, and still has a copy of the check from Warner Bros. But, like many, her appearance ended up on the cutting-room floor.

Maxine started making kaleidoscope blocks with hexagons and octagons almost as soon as she began quilting. She was always fascinated by the variety of patterns that were produced and that still appeared to have no relation to the original fabric. It all started when she was making a quilt and had no background fabric to use. Nothing in her stash was right, and she couldn't go shopping because there was a man fixing her kitchen, and she couldn't leave until he was finished. The only fabric that really matched the kaleidoscopes was the original fabric, which is when she wondered why she needed a background fabric at all.

Since then, she has not been able to pass by these wonderful prints without wondering what they would look like as a quilt. Whenever she brings a quilt top to her local quilt guild, the members always know that it will have wonderful kaleidoscope blocks, and they are surprised if she brings any other pattern.

Great Titles
from 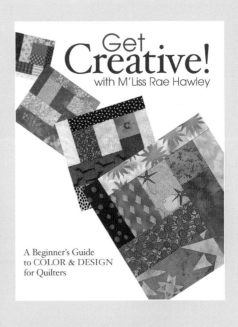 C&T PUBLISHING

Jan Mullen
Cut-Loose Quilts
Stack, Slice, Switch, *and* Sew

Easy & Elegant
LONE STAR QUILTS
All the WOW Without the Work!
SHIRLEY STUTZ

Get
Creative!
with M'Liss Rae Hawley

A Beginner's Guide
to COLOR & DESIGN
for Quilters

Nancy Johnson-Srebro
Stars by Magic
New Super-Easy Technique!
Diamond-Free® Stars
from Squares & Rectangles!
Perfect Points and No Y-Seams!

Free-Style Quilts
A "No Rules" Approach

Susan Carlson

THINKING outside the BLOCK
Step by Step to Dynamic Quilts

Sandi Cummings with Karen Flamme